BETWEEN TWO RIVERS

Tom Kins
October 2004

TOM KING'S
Sketchbook

BETWEEN TWO RIVERS
THE LOT AND THE AVEYRON
FRANCE

PUDDINGBAG
PRESS

For Lucy

First published in 2004
by Puddingbag Press

Tom King has asserted his right to be identified as the
author of this work in accordance with the Copyright,
Designs and Patents Act, 1988.

ISBN 0-9548132-0-0

Printed by Rhythm Consolidated Berhad, Malaysia.

CONTENTS

Hello Sir

My mother has just told me about your presence in the area (she likes it when things happen around her house!) and I would be most grateful if you could please leave a business card or some coordinates so that we could visit your exposition room.

My mom would also like to let you know that you can drop by any time and as often as you wish for a coffee or anything else. She is a very hospitable lady but don't worry: she won't be on your back all afternoon.

Thanks for honoring the area with your presence. Irish folks have a history of enjoying beauty and it is a compliment to this country than to have you here today.

good luck in your work

B. Collot

This wonderful letter was delivered to me by hand in the road where I was painting. It had been sent by fax from Bordeaux by the son of the woman who gave it to me. She could not speak English and I did not have enough French to converse, so she had asked her son to write the letter to tell me how pleased she was that I was there.

INTRODUCTION

On a beautiful September morning my wife and I boarded a ferry at Dover and crossed the channel from England to France. In the bowels of the ship was a car full to capacity, a trailer with thirty years of married life condensed into an area two metres by one and a half, and a dog called 'Womble.' We had left all our belongings in store and were heading for the south-west of France on a journey with no particular end in sight. I had been offered an exhibition of my paintings in France and we had decided to take a year out. That, at the time of writing, was two and a half years ago

I had first visited the Tarn and Garonne region twelve years previously on a holiday with a group of friends. I had taken my painting equipment with me and a chance meeting had led to the offer of an extended return visit the following Spring. Out of that I put together enough work to form the basis of my first one-man exhibition and it had set in motion a course of events that

would change my life quite dramatically many years later.

Until that time I had never been to the south of France and apart from a trip to Paris as a teenager, I knew nothing of the country. The holiday had been booked by someone else and my first introduction was a few pictures in a brochure, and my language skills amounted to one word, 'Oui.'

It took just twenty four hours to become enchanted. It was the markets that did it. In England shopping was something to be avoided at all costs, in France it was a social event, a visual feast and a gastronomic experience. I spent the two weeks of my holiday painting. I would return many times over the intervening years so when my wife, Sandi, and I decided to spend some time in France, it was the obvious place to come.

We rented a house for the winter months knowing that we would have to move on the following Spring. The days were still warm and for a few short weeks we had our meals outside and sat on the terrace of an evening watching the sun go down, the heat still radiating up from the slabs underfoot, as Summer gradually gave way to Autumn. I began putting together a collection of my paintings, my wife settled down to getting to grips with the language and Womble settled down to doing what she loves best - chasing the postman. She at least had no linguistic hang-ups!

A friend loaned me a twenty-year-old French post office van called 'Beryl' to use as a mobile studio and after a few temperamental problems with her insides, we began to roam the countryside looking for subject matter. My first surprise came as I drove through countless villages when I became aware that most people would smile and wave to me. I was quite moved by this until I realised they thought I was the postman, so I learned to drive with a permanent smile on my face.

The days grew shorter, a fresh chill filled the space left by the setting sun, and far-off sounds drifted across the empty sky from distant places. Winter draped its cloak over the land, shutters were drawn, and we retreated indoors. My days were spent out in Beryl and my evenings around a log fire, reading. Gradually canvasses were covered in paint, sheets of paper with watercolours, and sketchbooks began to fill.

Winter is different here, it can be very cold but there is still light in the sky. Many of the trees retain their dead leaves throughout the winter; they cling to the branches on fragile threads resisting the strongest winds, only to lose their grip by the new shoots pushing through the following Spring. They cover great swathes of land and act like millions of tiny mirrors reflecting the low winter sun, picking it up and throwing it back in your face in a kaleidoscope of colour.

It is at times an enchanted place with fairytale chateaux that hang suspended in space, surrounded by mists that swirl up from the valleys below. Rivers have cut through the soft limestone over millions of years and left gorges weaving through the landscape, exposing the layers of time like some giant gateau sliced through the middle. Towns and villages that have defied gravity for hundreds of years cling to their edge, crumbling and mellowing, so that they become one with the fabric of their foundations.

In Summer the sun bakes the earth and serried rows of vines hang corpulent with the grapes that make up the Cahors, Quercy and Gaillac wines. Windows and doorways bleached by the sun display an array of plants in anything that will hold a root and soil. Buzzards hang on the thermals, red squirrels climb the trees and deer forage in the fields below the house where we live. When I first came here I longed for the Summer, the heat and the colour, but it was only when I looked back at the pictures painted over a period of time that I realised I was like a hungry man at a banquet who does not know when he is full and longs for the next course, but the main dish had already been served, and winter was the feast.

Much of the appeal of France however, has more to do with the lifestyle than the landscape. France has managed to hold on to many of those values that are important to a quality of life that has already disappeared in many parts of the world. A pace of life more in tune with our needs, taking time to relax, the family unit, a healthy disrespect for rules and regulations, the famous lunch. But there are changes, and as is so often the case, they are slow and gradual, but the accumulative effect is significant.

My observations are those of an outsider and many of the things I find interesting, exciting and different are perhaps ordinary, everyday events to French people brought up in the area. That is, I think, one of the great things about travel, one sees the world through fresh eyes. Much of my interest has focused on people and their interaction with their surroundings; sitting in a cafe, shopping in the market, playing boules, or the hand of man upon the land: the signs in the streets, the architecture, farm buildings, the bridges that span the rivers. Over a period of time as the country revealed more of itself, so I became aware of the many festivals that take place throughout the year, the street parties, customs and traditions. This is a personal sketchbook of those things in a particular part of France with which I have become familiar; they were not done in any order but as the mood took me, and on some occasions I just followed Beryl. They cover the area between the rivers Lot and Aveyron, and in particular the area between Cahors and St. Antonin-Noble-Val, although I have gone as far east as Conque and as far west as Puy-l'Eveque. Most of the illustrations are from my sketchbooks, some were done as preparatory works for more finished paintings in either oil or watercolour, and some just for enjoyment. Others are finished works in their own right. My aim has been to convey the everyday way of life, the mood and atmosphere, together with the more picturesque - seen through the eyes of an artist.

Some bring back special memories like the sketch painted just outside of Milhars when the temperature had been at minus fifteen degrees for some time, and the Aveyron had frozen over for several weeks. Beryl had no heater to speak of and huge gaps around the doors and windows, (I had been warned not to take her into a Car Wash as I was assured it was like sitting in a colander!). On other occasions it was like sitting in an oven hot enough to cook a cassoulet. Others remind me of people I have met and conversations engaged in where neither party could speak the language of the other. Such conversations can go on for long periods of time and despite the difficulties, a mutual understanding is reached. But then as one young woman pointed out to me at the reception of my first solo show in France, 'painting is a language, universally understood.' Some people have gone to extraordinary lengths to communicate: One woman in her frustration to speak to me phoned her son in Bordeaux, over a hundred miles away, because he spoke English, and asked him to send a fax which she presented to me in the road telling me how delighted she was that I was in the area painting!

It seems a lifetime ago since I rolled over in bed, more asleep than awake and said to my wife, 'Why don't we sell the house, put everything in store except for our clothes and my painting equipment and rent a house in France for the next twelve months?' The muffled response from under the covers was just audible, 'Sounds great, let's do it.' Nothing more was said for several hours.

9

The catalyst for this outburst was a phone call from a friend living in the south-west of France asking me if I would like to have an exhibition of my paintings there. We had been thinking of putting the house on the market for some time and moving on, but were undecided on the best course of action to take. I had moved to Norfolk with my wife just four years earlier to become a full-time painter after years of running two careers, and had finally given up the day job. We had purchased a small farmhouse and although my paintings were selling well, it had taken a long time to re-establish myself. The house needed a lot of work and there was a range of outbuildings, all in need of repair. We had considered various options but all involved borrowing a lot of money, which we were reluctant to do. Earning a living as an artist has never been easy and there are long periods of time with no income; what was needed was a fresh start.

Most of the major decisions I make in life seem to creep up on me and catch me by surprise, it is as though someone else has made them. I spend weeks and sometimes months ruminating over what to do, weighing up all the options and hoping there will be a sign - then out of the blue, the other me, the one that creeps around in my subconscious, sorts it all out. There is no discussion, no great moment of inspiration, just a gentle awareness that a decision has been made for better or worse, and it feels comfortable. From that moment on all other doors are closed and best left so, for to speculate on what might have been is folly. So it was that while I was busy weaving the jumbled spell of thoughts and emotions that we call dreams, the seed was planted in my head that this was a good idea and when I awoke, it was there. All I had to do was make it happen.

It was some time later, after a considerable amount of thought, that I raised the subject again. I am prone to wild flirtations of imagination which occupy my every waking hour for several days only for them to fade away like a politician's promise, but this was different. The more I thought about it the more I wondered why it had not occurred to me before. Regardless of the outcome it would be a wonderful year, renting would give us flexibility and I can take my work with me wherever I go. There were many things to consider - what to take and what to put in store; there were possessions we might need access to while we were away - a large collection of garden pots, my books, which I can only be prised from in extreme circumstances, a large hairy dog, and a cat. Credit cards would have to be paid off, special banking arrangements put in hand, the car would need to be in good order, and we would need extended health cover. The tax and national insurance offices would need to be notified, a re-direct put on the mail, visits to the doctor, dentist, optician, and my art materials which I would need to take. We would need to find a company to store the furniture, source a house in France with studio facilities, and begin the process of obtaining a passport for the dog.

The pet passport system had only just been introduced and many people were unsure of what to do, including the authorities. The idea of a passport for the dog conjured up a vision of some regal canine aristocrat travelling the world with a string of Louis Vuitton suitcases covered in international stickers. Womble is not that dog! She came from the local butcher, the progeny of a long line of in-breeding. Neurotic, insecure and frightened of her own shadow, she cost us £10. We were robbed - but the butcher threw in 2lbs of sausages to ease the blow! Described as a Collie cross she looked more like a small brown bear. We called her Womble because of the way she walked, and soon dicovered that her mission in life is to consume as much food as possible, rabbit droppings being considered something of a speciality. Womble is no lady - what she can't eat she rolls in, and visitors to the house are advised not to kiss her on the lips!

Undaunted by these problems we decided to put the house on the market and take it a step at a time. For a while life carried on as normal and we put distant thoughts of France to the back of our minds, it was for the time being out of our hands. We still had to cut the grass, prune the roses, deal with any repairs that came along, and earn a living.

We found a buyer for the house very quickly and then the serious business of putting the wheels in motion began. We decided to start with a good clear-out. Thirty-four years of married life is a long time to accumulate things, and there was all my work files and equipment. I lost count of how many trips I made to the tip. Local farmers were employed to come and take the larger items away and for weeks there was a bonfire consuming anything that would burn. Despite this there seemed very little reduction in our possessions and the list of items going to France was getting longer - so I went to see a man about a trailer. I decided to have one made thinking this would give me more flexibility, but after some time discussing dimensions and trying to visualise how much each would hold, it all came down to the most economical size that could be cut from a sheet of metal.

The legal side of the sale was progressing and we were slowly working our way through our schedule, it was time look for a house in France. Choosing an area was not difficult. I had been to the south-west many times as a result of one of those chance meetings that many years later changes the course of one's life, and it seemed an obvious place to start. The plan was to rent a house for six months and then move on with the intention of seeing some more of the country, so a phone call was made to Graeme. Over the years Graeme, and his partner Caroline, had taken a

keen interest in my work and made it possible for me to return to France many times to paint, and they had offered to find us a house. So, while Sandi stayed behind to continue sorting our affairs, I made a quick trip to France. Twenty four hours after leaving Norfolk I was driven up a dirt track just outside of Caylus. It was early Summer, the temperature was up in the eighties, and as we rounded a bend between open fields there, nestled in the shade of a group of trees against a backdrop of rolling hills, stood our home for the next six months. Pantiled, honey-coloured and French to its foundations. An empty hammock sagged between two trees and a stone table caught the rays of the late afternoon sun as the car bumped down the track, leaving a cloud of dust in its wake.

The house was perfect, it was larger than we needed but it had space for a studio, plenty of room for the dog to roam and was in a delightful position. In the Summer months it was let to visitors but it was available for the winter at a very reasonable rent. There was one small problem however, it would not be available until the second week in September, six weeks after the scheduled completion on the sale of the our house. As it turned out we would need all of this time to put our affairs in order.

The weeks seemed to fly by, more lists were made, more bonfires and more trips to the tip. I collected the trailer just three days before we moved but I was already aware that it was going to be too small. In the intervening weeks more things had been added to the list of items to go to France. Womble continued with her schedule of visits to the vet for her passport, the whole

process was so complicated I was convinced they were going to ask us to have her photo taken. I had visions of us trying to get her onto a swivel stool in one of those photographic cubicles while we drew the curtains and asked her to sit still and not to smile. Sandi said I was being stupid, 'How could they expect the dog not to smile under such circumstances!'

My work equipment presented the biggest problem, what should I leave behind, what would I need in the future? I opened the drawers to my desk and stared in at the jumble of clutter. I had tried many times over the years to throw things away but every time I emptied the contents out, they all went back in one by one, and the only thing to end up in the bin were the bits of fluff and dust that had collected in the corners. To the onlooker it would have seemed a motly collection, but time and I had put together a range of tools to perform every requirement of a graphic designer and illustrator. Many of these had become worn to the shape and angle of my hand, others worn smooth from constant use. Some had perfect balance so that they became one with my body, another limb. Each had a specific function, some only used once or twice a year, but they were there when I needed them. There were old tins full of nibs, tools for folding and creasing paper, special inks and anything that would make a mark. In the end I emptied the contents of the drawers into a cardboard box to go in the trailer. The same thing happened with the small chest of drawers containing my paints, it was easier to take them as they were. And so it went on.

At last the removal van arrived and despite our

efforts up to the last minute to reduce our possessions, it still took two days to take everything away. When the removers left my worst fears were realised, there was still a great pile of odds and ends to go with us. We had to leave them with a neighbour and make two return trips to Norfolk to collect them later. Condensing our lives to fit into a car and trailer was going to be no easy matter.

We locked the doors and took one last look around the property, we were sad to be leaving. 'Cold Custard Farm' as we had nick-named the house when we bought it, was not just a home, it represented the first step in changing our lives, and like all homes had seen happy and sad times. We peered in through the windows but without the furniture, the rooms had lost their personality.

Just as we were about to leave the cat turned up as if to say 'goodbye'. She had disappeared for a few days sensing that something was going on and decided to keep out of the way. 'Hebe' was everything Womble is not. She was of feral stock, belligerent, independent, grey-blue and beautiful; the offspring of the two cats who lived in the big piggery. The previous owner of the house, an elderly Norfolk man who had lived there for forty years, kept one of the kittens for us. Each time we returned to the house during the negotiations he would pick up the little ball of grey fluff and refer to the kitten as 'he.' One day Sandi asked him, 'Are you sure it's male'? 'Oh no' he replied, astonished, in a broad Norfolk accent, 'he be female!' And so 'Hebe' she became.

Hebe spent most of her time outside in the barns only coming in to be fed. In the depths of winter she would get into the cupboard beside the Rayburn and make herself comfortable where it was so hot, we often wondered how she could breathe. But she survived, and on many occasions forgetting she was there, gave us both a shock on opening the cupboard to be confronted by two green eyes (the only part of her anatomy visible) staring back at us from the deep recesses. We decided, very reluctantly, to leave Hebe behind with the new owners who had agreed to take over feeding her.

The trailer stood on the drive hooked up to the car, we stood there clutching the keys to the house trying to take in as much as we could; we knew we would never be coming back. We walked along to the kitchen window and looked in. A big farmhouse kitchen, we had filled it with as much colour as possible - hanging utensils, pots, pans, chopping boards and baskets on the walls, to cover up the plain white tiles that had made it look like a hospital. We had painted the cupboards and put up shelving which we filled with our collection of jugs and teapots. A large pine kitchen table had filled the centre of the room graced by four bright-blue chairs, around which many riotous family gatherings had taken place, and seasonal festivities had been celebrated. It was this same table that we sat round just a few months earlier with the estate agent, discussing the sale of the house.

It was time to turn our backs on 'Cold Custard Farm.' The garden was in full bloom waiting for the new owners to start the cycle over again. We had to drop the keys off with the agent and be on our way, there was still a lot to do and it would be another six weeks before we left for France.

13

England, Autumn 1999

It is a bright, sunny day but cold and damp after forty-eight hours of heavy rainfall. I took the dog for a long walk across the fields at the bottom of the lane and up through the woods. The fields were heavily waterlogged and in the woods the pungent aroma of matted, rotting leaves on the ground filled the air. We put up a pheasant, grey clouds of pigeons rose from the tree tops clapping their wings in thunderous applause, and mallard ducks rushed past in a classic V-shape through a reluctant blue sky turning to dusk. A group of yellowhammers had singled out one bush as a perch providing a welcome splash of colour to the sombre, winter landscape.

I stopped for a brief rest by an old tree. A bough, split away from the main trunk, provided a convenient leaning post; it ran out at right angles to the main stem and curved gently before lodging in the ground. The branch was just the right height and my body seemed to fit into its curvature like an old armchair. It was an old willow, there were several of them along the valley, they follow the brook that rushes past just a few feet away. The heavy rainfall over the past two days had turned what is normally a gentle flow into a rushing torrent, churning up the mud underneath and turning the water brown: every undulation and interruption reflected in the shape of the water as it eddies and flows, dips, curves and bubbles on its journey. A leaf, caught in the current, tries in vain to escape the rhythmic flow; it swirls around and gets sucked down, rises and repeats the action over and over again like a planet trapped in an orbit by invisible, magnetic forces.

I looked up into the tree and sky beyond, by now a deep blue; a jet, a mere spec to the eye left a white vapour trail stretched out behind it. The sun, now out of sight, splashed a pink glow across the horizon and for a moment I felt like the leaf, trapped by the forces of nature while the rest of the world sped by.

Our first home in France

A FRESH START
France, Autumn 2000

I was hardly aware of the sensation as the ferry slipped out of Dover harbour on a Friday morning while most of England was still asleep. The sea was calm, a gentle wave lapped the grey harbour wall and a rustly old anchor that stands guard at the entrance, slipped past the window. The white cliffs of Dover bathed in the early morning mist of a beautiful day ahead, looked more mauve than white, as we left England behind. Not much was said, we had breakfast and stared out of the window. We were both nervous, anxious and excited, each looking to the other for reassurance. We were thinking back and looking forward at the same time. There had been some tears at the last moment with the realisation that we would not see our friends and family for a long time. There had been a lot of excited talk about what we were going to do, but this was it, and there was just the two of us.

Below, on the car deck, Womble sat waiting anxiously for us in the car. She had the whole of

the rear to herself but elsewhere the car was packed to capacity. The last few days before leaving had been frantic. There was a strike by lorry drivers resulting in petrol blockades and long queues at service stations, together with rationing. We were desperate to conserve what petrol we had until we crossed the channel. I had packed and repacked the car several times, the last stages done in the pouring rain. In the end I had bought the largest roofbox I could find and with the help of two shop assistants, fitted it to the car in their car park.

The car rolled off the ferry at 7.15am and we began the slow drive down through France which would take two days. Womble bobbed around in the back, she hates the car and will not lie down, so every time I looked in the rear view mirror instead of seeing the traffic behind me, there was a large, brown face staring back at me swaying from side to side with the motion of the car. The back seat contained all the fragile items; hi-fi

15

system, television, radio, camera, a computer (which I did not know how to use), together with printer and scanners. The roofbox contained all our clothes and the trailer was filled with enough painting equipment to see me through a year - easels, lights for copying my work, shelving, twenty-four paintings, a tool box, books, tapes and an assortment of odds and ends.

At 5.00pm the following afternoon the car turned into the track that led to the house after a slow, but uneventful journey. The track climbs steeply for the first few yards and had been worn into two deep ruts from farm vehicles before dropping down to the house. The car, weighed down with all the luggage, bottomed out on the raised piece in the middle and became firmly stuck. I tried to pull away but the wheels just spun round and there was a terrible smell of burning. We had travelled almost a thousand miles with no problems and just a few hundred yards from the house, the car was stuck. Sandi suggested that if she and the dog got out it might lighten the load and they could walk the last few yards. I put my foot down and tried to steer the car up onto the ridge in the middle of the track. It slowly moved forward, wheels spinning, a horrible sound of crunching coming from underneath, clouds of dust and more burning. I was convinced the exhaust had been ripped off and the clutch burnt out, but that was tomorrow's problem, all I wanted to do was get to the front door.

Once over the hill the car rolled the rest of the way and I overtook Sandi and Womble a minute later. At the front door I got out, stretched, and looked around. The house was just as I had

remembered it. The September sun still had some power but was just beginning to draw lengthening shadows across the parched fields from a sky of duck-egg blue. The tinkling sound of dried leaves gently falling on the stone table was just audible, echoing the first stages of Autumn, and there was still some colour left in the geraniums hanging round the old oak barrel; we would eat outside tonight. In the distance Sandi rounded the bend with Womble running in front of her wagging her tail, glad to be out of the car. It was the first time my wife had seen the house.

The following morning, Sunday, we awoke to a bright, sunny day, tucked away a good breakfast, un-hooked the trailer and decided to head for the market; we could unpack later. The exhaust had survived, as had the clutch. We followed the road that hugs the river Bonnette hemmed in on both sides by cliffs and rolling hills covered in trees. Houses and châteaux normally hidden from view, peered out from eyries perched high above the road. In a barn a long table covered in a white table cloth was being prepared for a lunchtime feast.

The colour, the produce, the sights, sounds and smells, markets in France, and particularly the south, are always exciting. The echo from the stall holders bouncing backwards and forwards between narrow streets from shutter to shutter high above brightly coloured umbrellas, people with modern plastic containers queueing under aged-oak beams for wine from oak-aged barrels. People kissing, shouting, shaking hands, arms waving. Stalls overflow with the fruits of the earth, the greens are greener, the reds redder, the yellows brighter. Beans of fifty-seven varieties that had never seen a tin in their lives, fill rows of sacks, and cheeses of all shapes and sizes pervade the market with their aroma.

The trailer took no time to unpack; everything had survived the journey and the contents disappeared into the house so that I was left wondering what had caused all the problems. The next two weeks were spent sorting ourselves out. I was keen to start work as soon as possible so canvasses had to be prepared and a studio organised. Graeme loaned me an old French post office van to use as a mobile studio, which he called 'Beryl.' Beryl, who was bright yellow, was a temperamental old lady. She rolled when she moved and could leave a man numb below the waist if too much time was spent in her company.

When it came time for my instructions on driving Beryl Graeme believed in what he called the 'army method' of teaching - 'right, this is this, that's that, this goes here and that goes there, one, two, three - go.' He lifted the bonnet - 'now it's time to look at the engine'. I was at a loss to know why, I felt as though I was looking through her undergarments. 'Right, this goes here, that goes there, this is this, that's that, one, two, three-go.' Everything looked in order to my untrained eye. I drove Beryl home, the gear change was in the middle of the dashboard and I spent the journey trying to change gear with the door handle. Before I reached the house the dashboard lit up like a Christmas tree, I drove Beryl back. We looked through her undergarments again and adjustments were made. I drove her home again but there was no improvement, this time she was over-heating as well. The problem turned out to

be a broken fan belt.

I took Beryl out on my first tentative run and all was fine; I took her out a second time, we grew in confidence and began to travel further afield. We were getting on like a couple of newly-weds until the petrol tank got down to a quarter full and she didn't want to parlez any more. I decided to speak to her. 'Right, I do this, you do that, this goes here, that goes there, one, two, three - go.' Nothing happened. A new filter was fitted but as soon as the tank got down to a quarter full she began to struggle. I came to the simple conclusion that the answer was to keep her well topped up with petrol and whatever was going on under her bonnet was a private matter best left alone. After that everything was fine.

Beryl was a great asset. She rattled along in fine style rolling round bends and bouncing over bumps with enough noise to wake the dead. I developed an inverted form of snobbery driving her to the market on Sunday mornings, I felt as though I was becoming part of the local community. I decided to begin by exploring the Aveyron, an area with which I was already familiar, but the light changes everything on a daily basis and one can always find something new.

The Aveyron is a tributary for the River Tarn. Rising near Severac it forms the south-west boundary of the Massif Central and winds its way through the Aveyron Departement. It snakes through wild, deep gorges taking in a string of historic towns and villages on its way. Belcastel, Villefranche-de-Rouergue, Najac, Cordes, St. Antonin-Noble-Val, Penne and Bruniquel, to

THE AVEYRON

name but a few, before joining the Tarn north of Montauban. Along the way it creates some dramatic scenery - sometimes meandering, sometimes rushing through narrow, confined spaces in a torrent, tumbling over rocks with an angry roar. It shivers and trembles over weirs and stands almost motionless in quiet, dark pools where the river widens.

All rivers have their own personality and the Aveyron is no exception. In Spring it flows full and heavy from the winter rains past wooded hills splashed with the vibrant greens of the new year's growth. Falcons criss-cross the empty fields that skirt its banks looking for easy prey; there is no sign yet of the crops that will fill the market stalls with their produce, cellars with their liquor or barns with their winter's store. As Spring gives way to Summer so the russet colours give way to greens in every hue. Maize,wheat, barley, fruit trees, vines and tobacco plants fill the pockets of land scattered between the woods, and tall sunflowers with 'dinner plate' faces turn their heads to follow the sun, painting the fields vibrant yellow. The river is thinner now, slower, as it ripples over pebbles on its bed, the loud hollow sound as it passes under bridges has given way to a quiet whisper. People fish on its banks, canoe on its surface, swim in its cool waters; children paddle, and families picnic on its banks. Insects dance in the warm evening haze flickering in and out between the rays of light shafting across its surface.

Autumn brings other delights; walnuts, chestnuts and figs fall from the trees, strips of land freshly turned expose a rich, red soil and the landscape begins to change colour once more.

The morning sun warming the cool night air brings with it the Autumn mists that swallow up the land, draping everything in a veil of shifting particles and leaving behind a fine spray, with days that are warm and fresh. Trees beginning to turn shed a confetti of leaves across the river's surface and follow it down stream. The sweet smell of freshly cut grass fills the air and haybales lie scattered about the fields like huge dice thrown at random. Wild boar forage in the stubble and deer venture out from the safety of the trees to graze.

Winter is slow to come, but there is beauty here too in the emptiness and solitude. It is not usually until after Christmas that the bad weather sets in and the river begins to swell. The heavy mists now cling to the surface all day shifting and rolling, following the river down stream, an air-borne tide locked in its embrace. There is an ancient 'other worldliness' about the atmosphere as though one has walked through a secret door into a land of Wizards and Goblins; the surrounding landscape only revealing itself in its upper reaches and appearing to float on a shifting bed of vapour. A cosmos of stars fills a night sky black as jet, endless and uncontaminated by stray light. It reveals another world, older and more mysterious than our own, and as yet unaltered.

Travelling from Montauban in the direction of St. Antonin one's first impression of the countryside is of a flat plain and there is no indication of what lies ahead. It is not until one gets to Montricoux that things begin to change; suddenly the river Aveyron is on your left and the gorge begins to climb. Within a very short distance it towers overhead and suddenly

Bruniquel is above, perched like a bird's nest with commanding views across the country, a fair indication of a violent past.

It is hard to believe in today's peaceful environment, the unsettled history of these towns and villages that follow the Aveyron upstream from Montauban along the gorge, (the old valley route from Quercy to Albi). Attack could come at any time from any place and one's peaceful neighbour could, almost overnight, become your enemy. Cathars, Catholics, Protestants, Knights Templar, the Knights Hospitalier of St. John of Jerusalem, Hugenots, the Hundred Years War, the plague and personal rivalries between ruling families, have all had a part to play in shaping the landscape. The peasants in the main cared little

Suspension bridge over the Aveyron at Feneyrols

Brusniquel from the bridge over the Aveyron

The gateway to the
château at Brusniquel

for, and had no influence over these changes, but
were mere pawns swept along on the tide.

Penne is not untypical of the changes that
could take place. During the Crusades against the
Cathars the lords of Penne sided with the Count
of Toulouse who supported the Cathars as much
as he could and thwarted many invasions by
Simon de Montfort. The inhabitants of Penne
endured the Hundred Year's War between the
English and the French, changing sides as it went
along. In 1569 the Protestant army of Baron
Paulin Philippe de Rabastens invaded Penne, a
Catholic city, but it was freed the following year
by Blaise de Montluc. It was invaded again by the
Protestants in 1586 leaving the castle and village

Bruniquel left, built to watch over the valley route from Quercy to Albigeois; the old château was set on medieval foundations and became a residence during the Renaissance. The newer château was built between 1485 and 1510.

Montricoux below, with its old streets of 15th and 16th century houses and church of the same period was, in Roman times, a river crossing. The village grew during the middle ages but it was not until the beginning of the 19th century that the communal forest of Bretou was sold in order to fund a stone bridge to replace the existing ford. Montricoux has had a troubled history; once a stronghold of the Knights Templar and later the Knights Hospitaller of St John in Jerusalem, it remained Catholic during the religious wars but came under attack from the reformers in Montauban and in 1568 and 1573 the town was plundered.

The Romanesque church at Montricoux

The château in Montricoux right, houses a private collection of paintings by Marcel Lenoir who was born in Montauban and died in Montricoux in 1931.

in ruins. The inhabitants were given permission to rebuild their homes using the stone from the château and what is left is a most extraordinary structure cantilevered over the gorge. It seems to defy gravity and one cannot help but wonder why it has not crashed to the ground long ago.

The Aveyron is not a great river, nor is it particularly long but it has, on its journey down through time, passed by a landscape of beauty deep-etched by the forces of nature and the hand of man.

Moving to another country for a year is quite complicated; much of the infrastructure for a permanent stay has to be put in place and I found settling down to work quite difficult. Insuring the car, opening a bank account, registering with a doctor, setting up the computer and sourcing suppliers for various things, all had to be dealt with in the first few days. These simple everyday tasks become major hurdles in another language requiring careful planning, scanning phrase books and trying to anticipate what questions will crop up. Needless to say the ones you think will be asked never are, and the ones you never anticipate always emerge.

Registering with a doctor was just such a case; we had assumed there would be a receptionist to tell us we could not see a doctor for several days. It came as a suprise to find there was no receptionist at the doctor's surgery, just a waiting room full of people. On enquiring where we had to go to make an appointment we were told to take a seat. Assuming they did not understand our bad French we asked the question again, but the reply was the same. We were about to leave when we saw a man with a stethoscope and Sandi asked if he was a doctor. 'Yes' he replied in English. We were so relieved not only to find a doctor but one who spoke English we practically fell on our

I have painted Penne right, many times and can still find things to interest me in its changing moods. In Spring and Autumn it emerges ghost-like from the mist trapped in the gorge below, and appears to float above the village without foundations. On clear days it hangs cantilevered over the gorge and one cannot help but wonder why it has not crashed to the ground below. Legend says that the Château was built between 545 and 597 and the village began to grow around its walls in the tenth century to form a Castelnau.

The Plague Cross at Penne below, has a latin inscription at the base, 'A PESTE LIBERIA DOMINE' (Lord deliver us from the plague). Penne was struck by the plague on more than one occasion.

Winter sun on Penne

According to legend, St. Antonin who was martyred at Pamiers, was guided to this place in a boat by two white eagles. A monastery built in his honour in the eighth century became the foundation of the village which began to develop in the twelfth century. Strategically positioned the town prospered through trade with Italy, Spain and Flanders and its products were exported to England and the Netherlands. St. Antonin boasts one of the oldest houses in France built around 1150 which became the town hall in 1313.

St. Antonin reflected in the Aveyron

La Halle, St Antonin

Café society, St. Antonin

knees. 'You just take a seat, you may have to wait a little while but eventually I will come and collect you.' The system was so simple we could not help wondering why it was not like this everywhere.

Two weeks after our visit to the bank a cheque book arrived. Only then did we realise that we did not know how to fill one out. For a time every task felt like climbing Mount Everest but as the weeks went by we gradually slipped into our respective roles and felt more comfortable with our surroundings. We had agreed before we left England that Sandi would concentrate on learning the language and keeping body and soul together, I would learn to use the computer and concentrate on painting.

The computer sat on the desk for the first few weeks and I hardly dared to use it. It had been bought principally for comunication and although I had spent many years directing design work produced on the computer, and was well aware of its capability, I had never had occasion to use one myself. I was conscious of the fact that it could be useful in producing promotional literature for my work and keeping a database of my paintings, so I had invested in some very serious graphics packages and was starting at the complicated end. One week's training was all I had from my daughter, a designer, before she went off to live in Australia, after that I was on my own. It was just after Christmas that I began to use the computer for anything other than sending emails, and it was a very painful process. If we had not been living in a rented house I would have thrown it through the window on several occasions but gradually, as I got to grips with it, I

Arnac

Cazals

Feneyrols

There are many châteaux like the one above at
Feneyrols. They dominate the landscape of the
region - always majestic, the fabric of time etched
in their crumbling walls, and are of such convoluted
shapes that many look as though they might have
come out of a child's fairytale book. They peer out
from behind trees in open countryside and tower
over villages from the greatest vantage point.

realised that the studio equipment I had left in store was now available to me through the one-eyed monster sitting in the corner!

I taught myself to type and began writing again. My days were spent painting on location or in the studio, my evenings writing or reading. They were full and interesting, but more than anything they were mine to do with as I wished. As winter sank its claws into the land and scratched its surface with bitter winds, so other masculine skills of 'hunter gatherer' were required. The house had no central heating and the winters are very cold here. Two log fires and a gas heater I had brought from England were our only form of heat, so Monsieur Jacques became a regular visitor to the house. He had a farm down the lane

and had agreed to supply us with logs. We were astonished to find we were getting through a tonne every two weeks.

It was a very pretty house, long and low under a shallow pantiled roof in a delightful setting. Like many French country houses it looked large from the outside, but much of the property was made up of outbuildings and the house was quite compact. A large open-plan room occupied much of the ground floor containing the kitchen, dining and living area. There was a large fireplace at one end of the living area which had been filled

Typical Quercy architecture on the banks of the Aveyron.

30

in with a very efficient wood burning stove. The other stove was in the kitchen and was more like a bread oven placed on top of the work surface. I always considered this very dangerous and was frightened that something would fall out and set light to the wooden units underneath, but it was wonderful to have our meals in the kitchen with the heat from the oven at our backs.

The stairs to the bedrooms led straight up from the living area and the studio could be reached from a door in the kitchen which led through the garage to a room at the back. This

had once been a lean-to workshop and was in the process of being enclosed as part of the main house but the insulation was almost non existant, and being next to an unheated garage it was very cold in winter. Often I would stand working at my easel dressed in a thick, quilted chequered workman's jacket purchased from the local farming supply shop, and could see the hot breath coming out of my mouth despite the heater being on all day. It was a good sized room, north facing with double doors that looked out across fields and woodland, dropping down into a valley and up again to Lacapelle-Livron and the tiny church of Notre-Dame des Grâces perched on the edge of the hill. The winter sun lit up the tiny church like a beacon which could be seen for miles around.

We had been advised on good authority to have some Pastis in the house, as all French men drink it at any time of the day or night. Anxious to appear to be doing the right thing we duly bought a bottle and decided we better get some practice in as it is something of an aquired taste. After a couple of weeks we decided to invite Monsieur Jacques in for a drink on one of his log delivering trips. Until then unloading the logs was done in silence as he had no English and I no French. This situation had not improved much but we had become experts at drinking Pastis. It was 11a.m when he arrived and a look of horror appeared on his face at the suggestion. He was clearly wondering what kind of drunkards live in this house? We quickly rephrased the question and asked him if he would join us for a cup of coffee, and this he agreed to do.

He took off his boots at the door and we sat round the kitchen table, he in his stockinged feet, and the heat from the stove at his back. After the first few minutes we began to feel more comfortable with the situation and attempts at

Overlooking the Aveyron at Laguepie.

Seen from a distance, Najac rises out of the landscape like a volcano, with the river curving round at the bottom and the château erupting from its centre. It stands on the top like a decoration on a wedding cake, the village spilling out from it down the side of the hill, and can be seen from great distances. There are some fine old buildings in the village some of which are built on stone pillars. The château was built in 1269 and never lived in by a feudal family, but was occupied by a commander and his garrison. After the revolution it was sold for twelve francs and much of it used as building material. Nevertheless, it remains a very dramatic sight and must be one of the most stunning views in France.

The Pont Saint-Blaise on the Aveyron dates back to the thirteenth century.

Old world charm at Najac.

The château
at Najac

normal conversation were made. Sandi began to explain that she had started feeding a young horse down the lane with carrots and it now came to her when she called it. It would run after her like a dog and tug at her sleeve if she did not feed it. He replied that the horse belonged to him and he had witnessed these antics. Much was made of this with sign language, Monsieur Jacques drumming his fingers across the table imitating the horse galloping. We all laughed and a rosy glow appeared on our faces. Then Sandi asked if the horse had a name and he replied softly and simply, 'non.' Saying 'No' in France is normally a short, sharp statement made through the nose - final, to the point and without apology - but this was different. 'Then I shall call him Fred', she said with the air of John the Baptist. He nodded without expression and the deed was done.

A few days later we were recalling the episode to our friends who know the family, and they started to laugh. 'The reason the horse has no name is because they will eat it,' they told us, 'and their only son whom they dote on, is called Fredrick,' or as the French pronounce it 'Fred-er-ick.' Sensing our discomfort they decided to make the most of it and asked Sandi not to make the horse run too much as it toughens up the meat! The next time she took the dog for a walk down the lane she was surprised to see the horse coming towards her from one of the barns. He had escaped from his enclosure and was

Villefranche-de-Rouergue

Belcastel

The immense tower of the church of
Notre-Dame left, dominates the square
in the bastide town of Villefranche-de-
Rouergue. The Aveyron flows through
the centre of the town which became
rich trading in wool, lead and silver.
The Aveyron is also at the heart of the
pretty village of Belcastel, above right.

helping himself to the hay that had been stored
for the sheep. She had no trouble persuading him
to follow her using the carrots she had brought
with her but she had to endure constant nudging
and biting on the back of her jacket for more
supplies. As she approached their house Madame
came rushing out with cries of 'Jacques, Jacques,
Fred-er-ick est dans la route!' Clearly they had
decided to adopt the name and from that
moment on Fred-er-ick was no longer on the
menu! After helping Jacques to get the horse back
into the field Sandi was rewarded with six farm
eggs for her trouble.

38

THE LOT

Three slim towers, six gothic arches and diamond-shaped buttresses, form the fourteenth century fortified bridge of Pont Valentre at Cahors, left. It was built in a style brought back to France from the Orient by the Crusaders, and is the city's pride and joy. There were once three great bridges in Cahors, another of the fourteenth century and one even older - the Pont Vieux, with five towers. The Pont Vieux was pulled down in 1868 and the other in 1907 to be replaced by cast iron. It must have been one of the great cities but is still an exciting place to visit with plenty of interest.

MOVING ON

The Lot is a tributary of the river Garonne and has its source in the Lozère, but it too, has its tributaries, the Truyère and the Célé to the north. It flows on a course of deeply winding loops and like the Aveyron it passes between thickly wooded hills, gorges and rich farmland. The Lot is the larger of the two rivers and is perhaps the more stately. Here, too, ruins crumble gently and towns and villages cling to the rock face commanding stunning views over the valley, probably the most notable of them, St-Cirq-Lapopie, is reputed to be one of the prettiest villages in France. The abbey of Conques to the east was a major site on the old pilgrim route (the Via Podiensis) to Santiago de Compostela in Spain and the area is steeped in history.

To the east of Cahors the river meanders through a landscape of small vineyards, orchards, fruit farms, cereal crops and pasture. There is a sleepy, unhurried feel, and in summer the fields are punctuated only by the occasional couple working their land. Protected from the fierce heat of the day under straw hats, their skin aged a roasted brown, they move between the rows of crops often bent double for several hours. In the villages old women dressed in black talk or sit on balconies in the afternoon shade watching the world go by. Small groups of men cluster under a spreading tree in the public square or play boules on the dry, dusty earth. Long silences punctuate conversation, their movement is slow and the occasional chink of the metal balls crashing into each other is not enough to disturb the tranquillity of the moment. Small lizards scatter in a staccato motion over hot paving, stopping every few seconds to lift one foot from the ground. The rustle of leaves, the drone of bees and from time to time men in lycra, skin tight, steamlined and displaying all the colours of the rainbow, will sweep through the village like a comet: new-age travellers on two wheels with twelve gears - head down, pedalling hard and talking amongst themselves oblivious to their surroundings. The only other sound of their being is the smooth whisper of rubber rushing over wet tar: then they are gone - racing against time and leaving the old world where it was, to count the seconds that pass so slowly.

That same slow process eases the seasons one into the other. The days remain warm and bright but the sun rises just a little later on the horizon every morning as summer gives way to autumn,

Old houses on the Lot at Cajarc

41

I like Cahors left and below, it has style and a comfortable feel with broad tree-lined streets, squares, pavement cafés and the light of the south. Situated on a loop of the Lot which almost encircles the city, it was once the capital of the old kingdom of Quercy. A natural crossroad both on land and water, Cahors became prosperous under the Romans exporting wine and linen throughout the Roman Empire. It was through banking in the middle ages however, that it gained its wealth; it became a centre for the Templars and a seat of learning, the most important of which was the university founded in 1332 by Pope Jean XXII, a native of Cahors. During the Hundred Year's War when the British took possession of all other towns in Quercy, only Cahors resisted, protected by its dominant position and fortifications. Wine has always played an important part in the commercial life of Cahors and it is for this that the city is most renowned today. The market on Saturday mornings is well worth a visit - full of colour and local produce.

The statue of Gambetta below, who came from Cahors and defied the Prussians in 1870, dominates the main square beside cool fountains.

The theatre Cahors painted on a very hot day in July.

Place de Daurada, Cahors

and slowly the temperature begins to drop. Mists fill up the valleys, leaves fill up the gutters and winter produce fills the markets. Layers of flat grey fading off into the distance like a child's pop-up picture book replace the rolling hills, slowly revealing themselves to a sun bursting through a bright-yellow haze for a day as fresh as a minty toothpaste. Tractors plough their furrow exposing the earth like a tin opener opening a tin of beans, turning it over as if summer itself had been buried for another year. People retreat indoors and outwardly the villages die until the following Spring.

To the west of Cahors is the wine region which produces the grapes for the famous black wine of Cahors. A narrow strip of land on the south side of the river which runs through to Fumel, it is perhaps this more than anything that sets the two rivers apart. The soil is chalky giving a parched look in places but it is a beautiful, fertile valley, ancient and established. The river is wider here and in less of a hurry. Vineyards straddle the narrow road with neat rows of vines and wine châteaux display signs of their produce inviting one to come in for a tasting.

Christmas came and went almost without noticing: it is different here, none of the usual commercialism and on Boxing Day everything returns to normal. I found it too quiet and for the first time since arriving in France missed family and friends. Our daughters came out to see us the week before and we tried to re-kindle the old family festivities but it was not the same. The New Year on the other hand, came in with a bang. Sandi was rushed into hospital on the 2nd of January with a mystery illness and spent the next eleven days there. It was one of those situations you consider but hope will never happen. Most of our friends were away and I felt alone and vulnerable. It was a very worrying time and I was glad we had taken the trouble before we left England to organise all our health cover. We also discovered why France has the reputation for the best health care in the world. Sandi went to see the doctor at 11.00am and by 3.30pm that same afternoon she had been examined by two consultants at the hospital, and admitted. She was put into a private room with en-suite facilities and immediately hooked up to three drips. Despite the problems the experience had its lighter moments as well. In true French style the three course lunch came with a two-thirds bottle of red wine and the same again with dinner in the evening. No questions were asked about how we would pay for the treatment, health care came first. Only later when the situation had been stabilised was the subject raised.

The early weeks of the New Year were preoccupied with Sandi's health problems but I tried to focus on the forthcoming exhibition. I stayed indoors as much as I could but struggled to keep the studio warm and often had so many layers of clothing on I found it difficult to paint. A light dusting of snow covered the land and for a time it seemed that all I was doing was gathering logs and cleaning out fires. Despite the interruptions the body of work was growing and before I knew where I was the landscape began to change once more, emerging as if from a cave - fresh, bright, crisp and cleanly washed. A hint of blossom appeared on trees, fresh shoots pierced the ground and a sense of expectation filled the air; we threw open the shutters to let the light in and dreamed once more of warm days and meals outside.

The onset of Spring however, brought with it the propect of another house move. The lease on the current property was due to finish in the middle of May and a new home had to be found.

This problem was quickly resolved after an introduction to a builder who was renovating a house in the nearby town of Caylus, which we agreed to rent. We carried on with our lives feeling safe in the knowledge that things were falling into place and looking forward to the prospect of living in a town for a change. Meanwhile, we continued to make plans for the exhibition that would take place in June, but events were about to overtake us. Six weeks before we were due to move we received news that there was a problem with one of the main walls in the house which would delay the work by several months.

Laroque-des-Arcs

Set on a precipice with half-timbered
houses in narrow streets and steeply-
pitched roofs overlooking the Lot
100m below, Saint-Cirq Lapopie
above, is one of the most dramatic
villages in France. In the Middle-Ages
it was divided between four feudal
dynasties, the Lapopies, Gourdons,
Cardaillacs and the Castelnaus and
was the main town of one of the four
viscountcies that make up the Quercy
region. Because of this the fortress
was made up of a number of châteaux
and towers overlooking the village.

The post-impressionist painter,
Henri Martin, stayed in St. Cirq and
Andre Breton, the surrealist poet,
wrote here. The view from the village
of the river far below winding its way
through the Lot valley is breathtaking.

The situation was serious, the holiday season was about to start and most of the properties would already have been booked for summer lettings. We considered briefly the prospect of returning to England but there was still three months to go to the exhibition - going back was not an option. Sandi suggested printing some notices and placing them around the region, we had begun to know a lot of people in the short period of time we had lived in France and made some useful contacts. The French dictionary was consulted and the following notice appeared in shops, tourist offices and public places...

'URGENT. *Artist travelling with wife and dog seek furnished house to rent for six months.*'

Much to my surprise we began to get a response almost immediately. The first was from an English couple who had lived in the region for some time and had a large property, part of which was let during the summer months. The house faced inwards and was approached through some large wooden gates. Once inside it had the feel of a Roman villa with a central courtyard enclosed by buildings and a balcony at first floor level. The appartment was to one side of the quadrangle and was approached from the balcony. To the rear there were wonderful views over the property to open countryside beyond. The appartment which would have been fine for a two-week stay, was small and there was nowhere to work. The owners did kindly offer to let me use part of one of the barns which they offered to clear out, but there was another problem - they already had one booking for the summer and we would have to find somewhere else to stay during that period. We sat on the balcony with a cold drink enjoying the spring sunshine discussing the finer points with the owners and during the course of conversation it transpired they had a part-time job. They did garden maintenance for people with second homes in the area and one of their main clients was the local nudist camp! Despite the

Springtime at Cénevières on the Lot. The meadow in the foreground was beginning to fill with wild flowers and the gentle trickle of the water passing over the sluice gate was a delight to the ear.

49

obvious appeal of some part-time work for myself there were too many problems to overcome, and I could not persuade myself it would be suitable. I must be getting old!

The second response came from a French couple who had a small enterprise producing organic vegetables and herbs, who were in the process of renovating a farmhouse. They were living in a Pigeonnier on their land which they now wanted to let. We were greeted by a man who was tall and slim with the complexion of someone who works outside, in his mid-fifties, talkative and charming. He spoke a little English and as is so often the case with people who can speak another language, was pleased to have the opportunity to use it. So our conversation progressed into a situation where sentences start in one language and finish in another. This is something we had become used to and at times it

The Cardaillac ruins at Montbrun left, occupy a prominent position overlooking the Lot up river from Cajarc. Montbrun is typical of so many sleepy villages in this area, each with its own story to tell yet quiet and almost unaware of their past.

The suspension bridge below, crosses the Lot at Cajarc on the border between the Lot and Aveyron Départements. A previous bridge built to cater for the pilgrims of St. Sacrement visiting the church was destroyed in the Hundred Year's War.

One of the many suspension bridges that span the Lot.

almost becomes a language in its own right.

Before looking around the property we were invited to have coffee and Monsieur B explained to us that he had been in the merchant navy all his life before he and his wife had bought the farm. 'We are not from this country', he told me, 'We are from the north'. I thought he meant Scandanavia but he meant the north of France and was referring to the region. He explained that the first thing he did when he came to live here was take off his tie which he wrapped around his watch and mobile phone, and put them all in a cupboard where they have remained since then.

The kitchen had the feel of people living in temporary accomodation. There was a computer to one side surrounded by lots of paperwork and it was obvious this was also the office, but it was clean, comfortable and homely. We were shown round the rest of the property which was full of character and taste. The pigeonnier was the classic 'mules foot' design, a tall square tower, each room of which filled the internal space, one on top of the other. An attractive wrought iron railing made by the local blacksmith graced the staircase as it rose through the three levels to the final floor where the pigeons used to have their access in and out. The original openings had been retained but inside everything had been made modern and ship-shape - it had style.

We were then taken outside to meet all the animals; first the geese, then the hens, next the donkeys - we had already met the dogs when we arrived. We were shown the farmhouse that was being renovated, the lower walls of which were the original cliff face - it was easier to build onto it than remove it and start again, a process that is not that uncommon in these parts. We went into the polytunnels, inspected the plants, picked herbs from the ground which were crushed one by one so we could smell them. We were asked the English name for each one and were told the French names in return. At one point Monsieur B stepped over an electric fence and I was beckoned to follow. I looked at him, he was considerably taller than me, I looked at the fence. 'It's all right, I think it's off', he said nonchalantly. My eyes watered, what if it's not, I thought - I'm not sure how high I jumped but I cleared it with ease!

Sandi and I thanked him for his time. 'That's alright', he replied, 'my time is my own now, if I want to stand and talk, then I do.' We agreed to speak again in a few days and it was made clear to us that regardless of the outcome of our discussions, we should remain friends and greet each other when we met in the market.

We looked at several other properties, some would become available too late, or were too expensive; others were in the process of being rebuilt and a few we were unable to find! We had more or less decided to take the pigeonnier but put off the decision until the following week-end as I was concerned about it having no studio facilities and the limitation of a six month contract. On the other hand we were running out of time and there were a lot of advantages to our living there: it would be very good for our language to be with French people, and they were a charming couple; it would be a wonderful environment for us and the dog, and Sandi enjoys being surrounded by animals. We agreed to telephone them on the Saturday evening.

At lunchtime on Saturday the telephone rang, it was the owner of a small hairdressing salon Sandi had put one of our notices in. She told us a French client had just been in asking if she knew anyone who wanted to rent a furnished house. 'Its a farmhouse in a wonderful position and the rent is very reasonable. You should contact her immediately.' We did, and the owner must have wondered what had hit her. We asked if we could

History, beauty and drama come together in a remote corner of the Lot at Conques. In a land full of suprises, this has to be the most enchanted place.

meet her at the house that afternoon and although it was obviously incovenient, she reluctantly agreed.

As we approached the house I said to Sandi, 'Surely this can't be right, I know this house, or rather I know the barns, I have often admired them when I have been out looking for subject matter to paint and wondered what was up here.' We turned off the small country road into the track leading to the farm past the large wire cages that stored the animal feed and climbed up past two barns on the right. At the top the track came to a halt in front of another barn and the house was off to the left. We climbed out of the car and looked around. 'Is this the right place?' I asked. The grass was overgrown, the shutters were all closed and moss covered the paving. It was obvious the house had not been lived in for some time and there was no sign of the owner. We looked around. The house was set in an elevated position and the land dropped away on all sides with wonderful views all around. It was a typical farmhouse of the south made of honey coloured stone, long, low and under a shallow pantiled roof. At one end there was an open barn with a traditional bread oven at the back, with the original wooden paddles for feeding the bread in and out of the oven lying to one side. At the other end of the house another barn was attached.

There was still no sign of the owner so we walked around the property. To the front the land dropped away steeply down to fields below planted with rows of vines, before rising again to hills densely covered in woods. Just off to the right were the stone barns we had passed coming up the track. One looked like an old coach house with arched openings, not typical of the region, the other was set on pillars but closed in on two sides. Both contained farm machinery which looked to be in use. Behind the barns looking down the track and beyond to the east, were more fields and densely wooded hills in the distance. At the opposite end of the house looking west towards St. Antonin, the view took in the valley and cliffs of the gorge. The gorge dropped away almost immediately behind the house and one had the feeling of being up in the treetops. A clearing had been made between the trees and one could look over more fields to the village in the distance and the church, isolated beside the river, was just visible.

To the west of Cahors are the wine villages which follow the river on the south side all the way to Fumel. Douelle below, was once a port from which the wines of Cahors were shipped by river on flat-bottomed boats to the ports at Bordeaux.

Château St. Sernin right, is typical of so many that grace this beautiful valley. Vines follow the contours of every undulation drawing neat lines across the land.

Château St. Sernin

Living on the edge, Albas below, clings to the limestone face above the Lot.

Winter light - Albas

Parnac – early Spring

We could not see inside but I had already decided this was the house I wanted. After almost half an hour however, there was still no sign of the owner and we came to the conclusion we must be in the wrong place, it was too good to be true anyway. We returned to the car and had driven almost to the bottom of the track when a green Golf turned quickly in beside us. Madame wound down the window and explained she had been waiting for us at the hairdressing salon. We apologised for the misunderstanding, turned the car round and followed her back up the track.

She was in a great hurry and opened one

shutter on the front door went inside and opened a shutter to one of the windows in the main room which, from what we could see in the dark, was a large living/dining room. In the gloom we could just make out the kitchen area at one end. She repeated the same excerise at a whirlwind pace in all the rooms which were viewed in semi-darkness. We asked a few questions and almost immediately found ourselves back outside again and the door locked. She then began speaking to us in rapid French like bullets coming out of a machine gun, but through it all we managed to decipher that someone else had already looked at

Winter vines at Pescadoires close to Puy-l'Evêque.

the house and had expressed an interest in renting it but could not confirm until the following Tuesday. We were also told that the house had to be rented for a minimum of one year and that all negotiations had to be dealt with through the Notaire in St. Antonin who was handling the property. She shook hands, said goodbye, got into her car and drove away. We looked at each other - what about the donkeys, hens, geese, the herbs, coffee on the terrace and the nudists - where were the nudists?! I still wanted this house.

It was 5 o'clock on Saturday afternoon and Sandi suggested driving to St. Antonin to find out where the Notaire was in preparation for our visit. Much to our surprise his office was still open and although it was pointed out that we should have made an appointment, the Notaire would see us now. After a few minutes we found ourselves sitting in two armchairs on the other side of his desk. He knew the house but had not been informed that someone else was interested in it; he would make a note of our name and address should they change their mind and would telephone us on Wednesday. On the way home as we followed the winding road that hugs the river Bonnette, Sandi was very concerned. 'What have we done? We only came here for a year, this will mean staying another year, can we afford it?' 'All we have done is register our interest in the property, we will worry about that when the time comes', I replied.

There was no telephone call on Wednesday, nor on Thursday, so on Friday Sandi rang the Notaire. When she put the phone down she turned to me and said, 'I think the house is ours.' 'What do you mean you *think* its ours?' 'Well he spoke so fast I couldn't understand everything he was saying.' 'We need to know, can you call him back?' A second call was made and this time there was no mistake. The house was ours!

57

THE LAND BETWEEN TWO RIVERS

The production of wine in the region has always been an important part of the economy. Cahors, Gaillac and Quercy wines are the main appellations and although all three are produced in close proximity, they are all very different in style.

The black wine of Cahors as it is known, is perhaps the most famous and its production predates the Roman occupation of the region. The name comes from the Malbec grape that produces ink-coloured wines and at one time it was preferred in England to the wines of Bordeaux, whose producers tried to block its transportation through their ports to protect their own trade.

Most Cahors wines come from the vineyards on the south side of the Lot to the west of Cahors. This beautiful fertile valley of red soil scattered with limestone pebbles forms a narrow strip of land that runs all the way to Fumel. No less attractive are the rolling hills a little further south that produce the Cabernet Franc, Merlot, Cot and Gamay Tannat grapes for the wines of Coteaux du Quercy. Panoramic views on all sides of scattered vineyards and farmhouses amid more open country with sleepy villages and scattered

woodland, make this a very pleasing landscape.

Further south the vines that produce the wines of Gaillac are among the oldest in France, some having avoided the Phylloxera epidemic that devastated the vineyards of Europe in the late nineteenth century. One variety, the 'loin de l'oeil' got its name from the translation 'Len de l'el which means 'far from the eye', (an eye in viticulture is a bud) because the bunches of grapes are suspended on a long peduncle. This old variety is only found in Gaillac. Despite the age of these vineyards it is only in recent times that the wine has regained its popularity.

Today the harvest of the grapes is mainly done by a machine designed to move between the vines that not only collects the grapes, but also crushes them ready for the vats. These large, expensive specialist pieces of equipment are usually purchased as a cooperative, each producer waiting his turn as each grape variety become ready for the harvest.

There are still occasions when the traditional picking of the grapes by hand is necessary and although a tedious job, much of the tedium is taken out by the good humour and collective spirit that abounds. The two sketches on this spread and the one on the previous spread were done over two days, the latter very hot. With a board fixed around my neck I followed the workers through the rows of vines sketching as I walked alongside them. Trying to keep everything balanced including a small pot of water, and work at the same time in the extreme heat of that early October day was not easy, but it made a delightful change to be part of a group of people working in the fields and share in a collective activity. The sun-dried loose soil sprinkled with limestone

A tight squeeze for tractor and trailer

Hot, dusty work gathering in the harvest.

pebbles underfoot, made walking difficult, and at regular intervals one had to duck between the wires to the next row in order to avoid the tractor coming to collect the harvest, for which there was only just room. But to lift one's head every so often to peer out from under the brim of a straw hat speckled with sunlight through the open weave, and look down the rows of vines scored across the valley like corduroy to the vineyards beyond, and the village steeple set in a blue haze, is a delight. To sit in the shade of an umbrella or tree, have lunch and share conversation, stretch out on the grass in the middle of the afternoon for a cool drink and feel the earth under you and the sense of space around; to breath clean air and look at the view through half-closed eyes and contemplate the wonder of it all, these are things no machine can replace.

The last days of summer at le Riols

The vernacular architecture of the area is, I feel, one if its greatest assets. The scene above could be almost anywhere in Europe but for the shallow roofline of the house in the distance and its blue shutters, which place it firmly in the South of France. The Gariotte right, once used by shepherds and for storage, is a clever construction made completely of stone with no mortar between. They are to be found isolated about the countryside and were a good way of using up stone scattered about the fields which, was also used in the making of dry-stone walls. The louvered windows of the tobacco barn opposite, used for drying the leaves, is a reminder of an industry once more prominent in the region.

Gariotte

Tobacco Barn

The paintings lined the walls of the studio, months of work on paper and canvas. Beryl stood on the drive ready to spring into action if required but her job was done - it was time to find a picture framer. Sourcing new suppliers is one of the frustrations of moving to another country, everything needed is here, knowing where to find it is another matter. After a few false starts I found a good framer so the car was loaded up with paintings and we set off with the French dictionary. I tried to anticipate questions so a list was made of key words: moulding, mount board, lighter, darker, too heavy, thicker, thinner, softer, how much? I agonised over each frame - had I made the right decision - but in time the framer began to get a feel for the syle I wanted and made a contribution to the decision making. So it was that one by one my paintings were given a number and a code and the next time I would see them would be behind glass or some expensive moulding. There was no turning back, the posters were already up in the streets and the invitations had been sent out.

The studio seemed strangely empty without the paintings but there were other things to occupy my mind. Before long we found ourselves back in the two armchairs in front of the Notaire, this time the owner of the new property was there too. We had not seen the house since that first visit but I had not changed my mind. The Notaire addressed Sandi and I and began to read the contract; the only thing I understood was our two names the rest was a verbal blur but I nodded sagely. He then turned to the owner and read her part of the contract, we then all signed. There was some laughter and the atmosphere was relaxed. The date of the move was set for the opening day of the exhibition so we explained the problem and it was agreed we could move in the day before. We all stood up and moved towards the door, shook hands, said goodbye and as we were about to leave asked Madame if it would be possible to visit the house again before the move as we had only seen it the once. 'Yes, of course', she replied, 'we are all going there now!' So out into the car park we all marched, got into our respective cars and followed Madame to the house. We had no idea why we were all going but it soon became clear.

Loze

Varaire

Jambluse

Traditional lavoirs shown here, have been preserved
in many places throughout the region and are a
delight to see. Originally the communal washing place
for household laundry, they vary a great deal in size
and style and now provide habitat for wildlife.

Between Vidaillac and Limogne

Lacapelle-Livron

This time all the shutters were thrown open and we could see the interior clearly for the first time. The Notaire walked round with a clip-board and pen and every time he found a fault he would tap it with his pen to draw Madame's attention to it and make a note of it on his clip-board. He

opened the cupboards and drawers and peered inside. 'How many forks are there, how many knives, spoons, plates, cups, saucers?' the Notaire asked. She did not know, she would count them. The process was repeated upstairs and then everyone went outside. Madame removed a slab

on the ground under which was some old sacking, polystyrene and plastic sheeting. She peeled away each layer exposing a large hole in the ground, stood up and looked at me. I turned round, all eyes were on me; the Notaire nodded to the hole in the ground, I looked down again,

Winters can be harsh. The sketch to the left, was done on a day when the temperature dropped to minus fifteen degrees and the river Aveyron had frozen over for the fifth day in a row.

67

Farm life — classic Quercy architecture in the fields around the region.

all I could see was a pipe at the bottom - I looked back at him. He nodded toward the hole again and it was obvious there was something I had to do. I knelt down and peered inside, I could see a meter on the pipe and then the penny dropped - it was the water meter and the reading had to be done by myself. Big smiles all round and a sigh of relief, that done we could all go home. The next time Sandi and I returned to the house, we would be moving in.

Quercy Farm

Lalbenque

Toulouse style or Mules foot.

Caylus

Cas

Penne

Much in evidence throughout the countryside Pigeonniers (pigeon houses) shown here, add greatly to the character of the region. Attached to farm buildings, standing alone in fields or incorporated into the structure of a house, many are architectural gems that have taken on a range of styles that far exceed their original purpose.

Domaine du Merchien

Cars lined the street outside, the car park was full. Inside it was crowded, the paintings hung on the walls and a long table was laid out with food and drinks. The exhibition was housed in the Maison du Patrimoine, which means House of Heritage, and there was a good mix of people, many I had never met before including some local dignitaries. I was introduced to the President of the Patrimoine and it became clear that he was going to open the exhibition with an introductory speech - it suddenly occurred to me that I would have to make a reply. Sandi and I mingled with the people making conversation and I looked around the room at the paintings in their new environment; each had its own story to tell or brought back some special memory. What had started out as a solitary activity and was originally a collection of individual paintings had taken on a new life, they were now a body of work - part of the story and a very public event. Eventually they would sell and take on another life; their new owners would not have seen the original subject, their interpretation would be through my eyes, and they would read into each painting their own feelings. Not for them the memories of being bitterly cold sitting in Beryl in several layers of clothing trying to get the feeling back into my fingers by wrapping them round a cup of coffee; or of being so hot it was impossible to use the watercolours because the paper dried before I could get a wash down. The miles driven, changing light and blinding sun, the people I had met and conversations engaged in. Nor would they know the warm summer days when the valleys pulsate with a haze and the droning of insects, when all was quiet but for the occasional car or tractor, and for a brief time the rest of the world did not exist.

The room was called to order and the President began his speech. I was suprised how many 'French' words I recognised - Guinness, whiskey, Irish music - perhaps this language thing was not going to be so difficult after all! It transpired he had been to Ireland the previous summer for a holiday and had loved it - he decided to use this opportunity as I was Irish, to share his experiences with the assembled crowd. Then it was my turn: my mind was full of mixed emotions, the fear of having to make a speech and the excitement of exhibiting my work in another country. I decided to borrow an expression from a young Dutch woman with whom I'd been having a conversation earlier, explaining how nervous I was feeling at having to speak in public. She told me, Painting is a universal language understood by all; you talk with your brush, the people will forgive you anything'. They did. It was a wonderful evening.

We had moved the day before the exhibition but were so busy had not had time to take in our new home surroundings. The move was easy but we had already accumulated extra possessions and it now required three trips with the trailer. The weather was good and we had the summer to look forward to. The house was a typical French farmhouse - one very large room containing the living/dining and kitchen area occupied the full width and three-quarters of the length of the ground floor area, with a huge inglenook fireplace at one end. The walls were of stone and those at the back of the fireplace were black from years of fires. It had been used for cooking as well as heat and all the implements for hanging the pots were still in place. A stone plinth had been built within the fireplace to raise the height of the fire and this presumably was so that cooking could be done in a standing position. A stone alcove about two

Set in the valley of the river Bonnette, Caylus is a lively medieval town with some fine examples of houses dating from the thirteenth to the sixteenth century. The market square was created in 1247 and the church was rebuilt in the fourteenth century. The château around which the original village was created was set alight in 1211 during the Albigensian Heresy.

71

metres long with an arched roof was set into the back wall of the living room with a stone sink at the far end, this was the original kitchen. The doors to the outside, both front and back, led directly off from the living room as did the open-tread stairs. The stairs were open at the top forming a gallery effect above the kitchen and the room had the feel of a baronial hall. At the opposite end to the fireplace an opening led to the toilet, bathroom and a bedroom. Upstairs there were two further bedrooms either side of a large landing area which looked down to the living space. The whole of the upper storey was open to the line of the roof exposing all the beams and the roof structure.

There was an air of neglect in certain parts and we began to discover that some of the essential items we needed were not provided. We had all of these in storage but it was cheaper to simply replace them. We cleaned up the house, rearranged the furniture and put in some of our own things. I had brought out some books and shelving from England and soon the place looked more like our home. We had wonderful views from all of the windows, and would later discover that the house had once belonged to the château in the village.

The owners had a business not far away growing vines which, were sold all over the world. They owned much of the land around the house and in time we discovered that the barns were used for storage for a brief period during the Spring and Autumn. The rest of the year we had the house and all of the surrounding area to ourselves. There is a wonderful sense of space living in an elevated position, it was something I had never experienced before.

There was no formal garden just an area of land surrounding the house, the grass had been allowed to grow very long and it took a considerable amount of time to get it down to a manageable level. A terrace ran the full length at the front with a smaller terrace at the back. A vine had been planted against the open barn but apart from that, nothing had been cultivated. Sandi put window boxes on all the window sills, cleared out a large stone trough full of weeds which stood at the front of the house, and filled it with flowers. This would be our home for the next twelve months.

St. Pierre Livron

Puylagarde

Verfeil

73

There is something wonderful about market days. Towns and villages that at other times are quiet and sleepy, become transformed, their mellow crumbling walls acting as a perfect foil to the brightly coloured umbrellas; the vibrant reds and greens of the produce in summer, the saffrons and browns of winter. The play of light falling between tall buildings in narrow streets that hold in the atmosphere, condense it, and squeeze every ounce of colour and noise until they become vibrant with excitement. Herbs and spices, spit roast chickens and the strong aroma of countless cheeses assail the nostrils. They are for me the embodiment of France, and I never fail to be moved by them.

The Monday market at Caussade

OPEN ALL HOURS

One Sunday morning six weeks after we moved into our new home we decided to visit the market in St. Antonin to buy two more pot plants and a baguette. We had planned to have breakfast outside at one of the cafés so we parked the car at the other end of the town and called in at the boulangerie to buy some pain aux raisins and croissants to have with our coffee. We had almost reached the café when I noticed a small shop for sale. We peered inside and I said, 'that would make a great little gallery.' It was just a throw-away comment and I meant nothing serious by it. It was dark inside and difficult to see the layout, it looked a little neglected but full of character with two large windows onto the street. The '*Avendre*' (For Sale) sign was hand-written and Sandi noticed that the owner had another shop just a little further up the street. It was a beautiful morning, the July sun was just clipping the tops of the buildings opposite as it penetrated the narrow medieval street - we were feeling good. 'Let's call in and see how much it is,' she said. It was only about 9.30am and Madame was clearly expecting the first sale of the day to be one of the dresses which she made, and seemed a little taken aback. She sprang to her feet, opened the drawer of her desk, pulled out a bunch of keys and within minutes we were back at the shop.

Low benches provide the only comfort at the animal market in Caussade.

75

It transpired that the whole of the building was for sale and we struggled to keep up with her as she extolled its virtues. The shop area was small but interesting, some plaster was missing and it needed a coat of paint. Upstairs was a disaster and we were not allowed to go to the top floor because it was dangerous. On the way back down I said I would not be interested in buying the building but would she consider renting the shop for a year? *'Oui,'* she said without hesitation, and told me what the rent would be immediately. We stood in the doorway, she had one foot on the step and an arm against the frame of the door; her long flowered skirt swept across her lower body and she reminded me of a figure from a Russell Flint painting. We asked what we would

The garlic stall — winter

The market at Limogne

The Sunday market St. Antonin

have to do to open a business in France. She lifted her shoulders up to her chin, puffed out her cheeks with a sigh, gestulated with her arm in a carefree manner which we took to mean 'just open and worry about that afterwards.' We thanked her and said we would come to see her the following Wednesday.

The market was in full swing as we took a seat outside the café and opened the bag containing the pain aux raisins. 'What have we got to lose?', I asked. 'The rent is very reasonable, if it doesn't work out we can just walk away from it - the rental period would tie in with the contract on the house. Besides we have a lot of paintings at home just sitting there.' I had sold some work at the exhibition but not enough to pay for the trip to France, and the money was running out. It might be fun. 'If we decide to go for it then we are going to have to make a decision quickly as we would need to be in by the end of July.' We finished our coffee and went back to the owner and shook hands on the deal. Madame reached back into the drawer of her desk and gave us the keys to the shop. That Sunday we went home from the market with two pot plants, a baguette - and a gallery! We had been in France for less than a year.

I had agreed to repair the broken plaster and paint the interior, we would need some display equipment and lighting - there was a lot to do in two weeks. I had also decided that everything should be done legally but nobody seemed to know what that entailed. It was the bank who eventually came to our rescue and pointed us in the right direction. We would need to go to Montauban, the commercial centre for this region, and were given the details of the organisation where we should register the business. We braced ourselves and set out on the journey. We found the building and the office and waited our turn only to be told, 'you are in the wrong place. You are an *artiste/peintre* this is where you would register if you were a house painter.' We were directed to another building and found ourselves before a young man who seemed a little surprised. 'But in France you don't need to register a business to paint'. We explained that we wanted to open a gallery and it was obvious it did not fall within the normal line of requests. He eventually found the right forms and within a very short time the deed was done.

We had decided that Sandi would be 'front of house' as she was the one with the language skills, and I would concentrate on painting. We were both very nervous on that first morning of opening but every day brought with it new experiences. Almost immediately we found ourselves mixing with different people and making new friends. Several of our fellow *commerçants* (business people) came in to welcome us and tell us how much they liked the gallery. Sandi's fears about her inadequate language skills were soon overcome when we discovered that the same conversations about the

paintings were repeated over and over again, so the vocabulary could be learned and gradually she grew in confidence. Every evening I would make sure I was at the gallery by 5.00pm in case anyone had expressed an interest in meeting me. I would feel a sense of excitement as I parked the car and walked down the narrow shaded streets between tall stone buildings and out into the bright sunshine; past the café in the Halle crowded with people, past the Coiffeur where there was always a cheerful wave from the two hairdressers, before turning into the street leading to the gallery. I knew before I arrived if there was anyone in the gallery because Sandi had got into the habit of putting her chair outside to try and catch the last few rays of sunshine, so if the chair was empty, then the gallery was occupied. She was always full of stories about the people she had met during the day and we celebrated every sale as if we had won the World Cup, even if it was only a card!

The gallery got off to a good start - we had sold the most expensive painting along with several others before the season came to an end in October. We knew that it would be very quiet during the winter months but it still came as a surprise at the beginning of September when the crowds disappeared almost overnight, as the majority of tourists returned home. The town slipped progressively into a pace of life more asleep than awake, the colours of the produce on the market stalls changed to the saffrons of winter and before we knew it, we were sitting down to our second Christmas dinner in France. We pulled the shutters across once more, Womble settled down by the fire and I put the trailer away in one of the barns.

I continued to delight in the location of the house as the seasons changed. The varied landscape brought a variety of wildlife much of which could be seen from the windows, or out walking with the dog. Perigrine falcons, hen harriers, red kite and buzzards, scan the field below the house. Deer, foxes and wild boar shared the same site at different times and the trees at the rear play host to red squirrels and many species of birds, so close one could almost touch them; wood-peckers, tree creepers, long-tailed tits, hoopoe and many others I didn't recognise. Along the river kingfishers skim the surface like iridescent jewels, and otters live in its banks. Some wildlife however, are less welcome than others. A creature referred to locally as a tree rat will venture into the house in winter. A very attractive animal with big eyes and a long bushy tail like a squirrel, its natural habitat is high up in the trees so they occupy the roof space of the house and can do great damage.

There were other unwelcome visitors: one morning Sandi opened the door and let out a

blood curdling scream when she saw a metre-long snake curled up against the door warming itself in the morning sun. I knew they were around and had watched them many times below the terrace at the back of the house where several of them live in the stone walls, but this was the first time we had found one so close. They are referred to locally as grass snakes, though they are nothing like any grass snake I have ever seen. Like most wild creatures they are more frightened of us than we are of them, but it is disconcerting to find them sharing the same living quarters. I was even more concerned when it slipped away into a crack in the open stonework of the barn attached to the house and I realised there were probably more snakes living there. On one occasion I watched two of them mating and it is one of the most hypnotic things I have even seen. Coiled together they moved in rhythm to music of their own making for some considerable time, each movement sensuous and expressive and I was reminded of the dancers of the east who use their arms and hands in a similarly sensuous way. Not all snakes are harmless however, and it is the much smaller vipers that are the problem. The real danger is to dogs who tend to be curious and rootle them out, and will die if bitten.

The year ahead seemed promising and we were looking forward to opening the gallery again at Easter - we had enjoyed our first experience and had found a sense of purpose for remaining in France. Then they began to arrive! We had obviously found our way on to a computer in Paris and bills began to arrive almost on a daily basis. We had no idea what most of them were for but they were all compulsory payments that had to be made to various organisations and I had not budgeted for them. Within a very short space of time the small profit we had made was gone and we were having to wrestle with another language - Beaurocracy! There were many occasions over the coming months when we almost gave up but once again the evenings began to draw out and somehow it seemed easier to cope with the problems when the sun was shining.

A makeshift stage at the Laguepie Chestnut Festival

82

Salsa

During the summer months there seems to be a festival for almost everything: Garlic, chestnuts, wine, walnuts, photography and many others. Towns and villages host elaborate music festivals featuring major international artists alongside traditional musical events. Theatre, dance, art exhibitions as well as cultural connections between France and other countries feature high on the list.

Jazz in the park at Foneyrols

It is only to be expected that in a region with
such a strong agricultural tradition that festivals
celebrating the history of farming will be
popular. This one at Espinas is typical with
demonstrations of old farming machinery and
working methods. The old steam engine took
a long time to get going but once working
was quiet and efficient.

Steam power at the Espinas Summer Festival

One day at the beginning of March Sandi said to me, 'I've been thinking about Lucy's birthday.' Lucy, our younger daughter, lives in Australia so we have to think about things like birthdays well in advance. Lucy's birthday falls at the end of May and has always been special as she shares the same birthday as Sandi and my mother. What to send Lucy is always a serious consideration as often the cost of postage can be more than the cost of the gift. The unexpected bills had left us short of money and Sandi's solution to the problem was to send her one of my sketchbooks. I gave this some thought but was reluctant to do it as I often refer back to them many years later. 'Why don't I scan my sketchbook of France into the computer and combine it with some of my writing about the region; it will give her an insight into the area where we live and I can make it up into a book?' We both agreed on this but it would mean my starting work at 5.00am every morning for several weeks to get it finished in time. So it was that 'Between Two Rivers' began.

The original idea was to do a one-off book but despite this there were many things to consider: The size of the book would be determined by the maximum sheet size of the computer printer, in this case A3: the number of pages by the binding process and the cover by whichever paper I could find heavy enough: I would have to précis the writing, always difficult for a person who uses fifty words where two will do! Each illustration would have to be scanned and all the back-

grounds removed - a very time consuming process. When this was finished I still had to get the pages to register back-to-back so that it would make up as a book. I decided to keep it as simple as possible and limit the number of pages to thirty-two, this way I could staple them together. I solved the cover problem by using watercolour paper which I folded over at the ends to give a double thickness, it also had a deckled edge which gave it a 'quality' feel. It was the sheet size of the watercolour paper that determined the final size of the book as I could get three covers out of a sheet. I printed the first sample books on ordinary paper but found it too thin so had to source a heavier stock, but then found the staples would not go through. It was now that all those special pieces of equipment I had brought from the drawer of my desk in England came in useful. The holes for the staples had to be pre-punched with a pair of dividers then the staples fed in and folded over by hand. If the sheets were not

perfectly lined up on the centre crease the staples would open when the book was folded. I made a label for the cover using one of the illustrations from the book which was cut out and pasted on. Despite the 5.00am start every morning I ran out of time and ended up sending Lucy the first marked-up proof copy for her birthday with a promise that the final copy would be with her in the next two weeks. In the meantime Sandi had taken one of the proofs to the gallery to check and three American women saw it and all wanted a copy. It was agreed they would come back the following Sunday and I would have them finished in time before they left for America. In desperation I started work at 5.00am on the Saturday morning and worked all through the night; it was mid-day on the Sunday when they were finished. Thirty-one hours without a break! I delivered the three signed copies of the books to the gallery more asleep than awake at 12.30pm - and two days later they were in America. The gallery had a new product and I was in the publishing business!

I had reserved the first copy for Lucy as promised and immediately began to make some more for the gallery. The process was painfully slow mainly due to the speed of the printer but the quality was very good and the finished item had a very professional look. Over the coming months I revised it a little making it slightly bigger and fine-tuning some of the text. Each book had to be cut out by hand with a scalpel and by high summer, when I struggled to keep up with demand, I felt as though I was getting through more scalpel blades than the National Health Service! We were forever running to the stationers for supplies and the art shop for paper. Little did I know at the time that for the next two years I would be making the books by hand on the dining table.

89

The contrast of the farmers and their dainty baskets displaying their precious crop, the curious red flag above the sign, the traditional costume of the truffle officials and the huge interest from the public and media; all these things make the opening of the Truffle Market at Lalbenque one of the most interesting and uniquely French events I have attended. Occasionally the handkerchiefs covering the baskets will be briefly removed and the object of all this interest seen, but no sales can be made until the red flag comes down.

The Chef de Truffes

MARCHÉ aux TRUFFES
OUVERTURE à 14ʰ30

Waiting for the flag to come down

90

The opening was due to start at 2.30pm I had been warned it was all over very quickly and was determined not to miss a thing, so armed with sketching equipment and a camera I turned up early for what I thought would be a bumper bonanza of colour. I had waited almost a year for the start of the Truffle Market at Lalbenque having missed the previous year's short season by only a week.

We parked the car at 12.30pm in an almost empty car park and walked the length of the deserted main street in this small village situated mid-way between Caussade and Cahors. There were none of the usual signs of activity associated with markets - no vans, no traders erecting stalls, no brightly coloured umbrellas, no noise. We began to think we had arrived on the wrong day but a row of scrubbed wooden trestle tables set up on one side of the street with a rope around them suggested something was going on. Behind the tables a sign with a small red flag stuck out from its top at a forty-five degree angle, announced that the market would open at 14h30. We looked up and down the street and were at a loss to know where everyone was. The market, I had been assured, was famous throughout France and is the most important in the south-west. People come from all over the country to buy the truffles, especially on this, the opening day.

We decided to call in at a café and have a coffee to kill some time. As we opened the door we were met by a wall of sound coming from the restaurant leading off from the bar. Rows of long tables heaving with people - noisy conversation, laughter, and cigarette smoke filled the air. Of course, it was lunchtime, and nothing interferes with lunch, not even a famous truffle market.

We took up a position at a table in the window and looked out at the deserted street on this bright, but cool December day, enjoying our coffee. Behind us toureens full of soup went backwards and forwards, wonderful smells wafted our way and I regretted the 'brunch' we had eaten before leaving home. I ordered two glasses of wine knowing nothing would happen before 2.00pm and opened a newspaper left on the table. Inside an article confirmed we were in the right place on the right day. It also told us that the depopulation of the coutryside and a less favourable environment had seen a decline in the truffle industry since the beginning of the last century - a familiar story. Production had dropped from 200 tonnes in the 1900's to between 3 and 10 tonnes today with the price determined by the abundance and quality of the crop which was currently selling for between 300-700 euros per kilo.

Some men began to appear behind the trestle tables on the other side of the road, each with a small basket placed in front of him covered in a brightly covered handkerchief. The street began to fill, and two men dressed in traditional costume started to play a melody of French music on the steps of the Mairie. Out of nowhere crowds began to congregate around the rope separating them from the tables, covered by now in an assortment of baskets. Each had its own chequered cloth concealing the contents, which could not be shown until the opening. Their owners lined up behind them staring out at the spectators who, in turn, stared back at them. Through the noise and excitement the strains of a familiar tune filtered through the sea of bodies and the Mull of Kintyre sounded as French as the Marseillaise before it was finally drowned out.

Television and radio crews from all the major stations began to walk between the narrow strip separating the farmers from the spectators, conducting interviews as they went along. Occasionally a cloth would be discreetly removed from a basket in order for a camera to film the contents. Not much to look at I thought, more like lumps of dried lava than a rare gastronomic delight, but a unique pungent aroma filled the air. A few farmers had bought two baskets but most just one, and each contained around ten of the precious truffles.

We began to get crushed against the barrier and I wondered where all these people had come from. I looked up to see people crowded on to balconies staring down at the spectacle. I turned around to see a television camera in my face and a microphone under my nose. I panicked, grabbed Sandi and stood her in front of the camera - I had put her on the spot and she had to endure a long interview in French. 'I knew I should have washed my hair and not worn this jacket', she said afterwards. 'Don't worry', I replied, 'they have interviewed so many people it is unlikly they will feature you.' Just then our attention was drawn to a procession pushing its way through the crowds. The Mayor, followed by two men dressed in long black capes, black hats and medallions around their necks, together with some other local dignitaries, walked to the steps of the Mairie and began to make speeches. It was impossible to hear anything that was said above the noise but eventually the speeches stopped. A whistle was blown, the flag above the sign came down, the rope around the tables disappeared and several hundred people converged on a few small baskets. The opening of the Truffle Season had begun.

Two days later while out shopping several people stopped us in the street - we were très célèbre. Apparently the interview had been shown in full on national television news!

Under starters orders

Before I came to France my life was 'between two rivers' - which one should I follow? Should I choose the safe, smooth passage and stick with what I knew, always wondering if I should have taken the chance? Or should I risk all, follow my conscience and go with the flow wherever it leads? The hardest part is letting go and although at times I envy the secure life of some of my friends, I would not want to lose the freedom I have now.

Travel brings many opportunities and other joys - just at that time of your life when you think you have seen it all before, the world begins to reveal itself as if through the eyes of a child experiencing it for the first time. Simple every-day events become something special, making yourself understood a sense of achievement, sharing a meal with strangers an honour. At times I have to pinch myself - is this really my life?

On that first day travelling across France with the trailer full of our posessions and Womble in the back of the car, we stopped overnight at Argenton-sur-Creuse to break the journey. The following morning at breakfast we were chatting to three Australians who later helped me hook up the trailer to the car. As we stood in the car park of the hotel in the bright morning sunlight they told us they had just been to Paris for a few days and were now on their way to Conque for a walking holiday following the pilgrim route to the Pyrenees. 'We thought we were doing something unusual till we met you guys,' one of them remarked. I had been so busy with the preparations I had not stopped to think it was unusual. It was their first visit to Europe and they had expected it to be more industrial and were pleasantly surprised to find they could drive for hundreds of miles and see little more than fields and trees. 'The world is still a beautiful place,' one of them said, and I agreed. We said goodbye, wished each other 'bon voyage' and set off on our separate journeys: the Australians on the well-trodden path established by the pilgrims in their search for truth hundreds of years before, and Sandi and I on our own personal journey of discovery - with no particular end in sight.

Thanks

I have received a great deal of help and support during the writing of this book from family and friends and would like to thank all those involved. In particular Graeme Hyde and Caroline Mackie for the loan of 'Beryl', Andrea White for her support and belief in this project, and special thanks to my wife, Sandi, who helped make sense of the ramblings of a fledgling writer.

Tom King was born in Dublin in 1946. He pursued a successful career in graphic design for many years, culminating in owning his own design practice. His love of painting in watercolour eventually led to a full time career as an artist and he has had several solo exhibitions of his work in England, Ireland and France. He has participated in numerous mixed exhibitions and has won awards for his painting. He is an associate member of 'Les Arts et Lettres de France' and in 2004 was elected a member of The Water Colour Society of Ireland. Tom and his wife live in the south-west of France where he continues to paint in both oil and watercolour and exhibit his work throughout Europe.